Exploring unmet need

The challenge of a user-centred response

Mary Godfrey and Gill Callaghan

The **Joseph Rowntree Foundation** has supported this project as part of its programme of research and innovative development projects, which it hopes will be of value to policy makers, practitioners and service users. The facts presented and views expressed in this report are, however, those of the authors and not necessarily those of the Foundation.

© Joseph Rowntree Foundation 2000

All rights reserved.

Published for the Joseph Rowntree Foundation by YPS

ISBN 1 84263 015 6

Cover design by Adkins Design

Prepared and printed by:
York Publishing Services Ltd
64 Hallfield Road
Layerthorpe
York
YO31 7ZQ
Tel: 01904 430033 Fax: 01904 430868 E-mail: orders@yps.ymn.co.uk

Exploring unmet need

Introduction

The concept of need is one of the most widely used terms in social and community care. It is also one of the most slippery to define. There is no agreement at a theoretical, policy or practice level on what it means or how it might be measured. Within the area of public policy also, need is understood differently in health and social care. Yet, a consideration of the meaning of 'need' cannot be left to the level of abstract debate, particularly since need and its satisfaction are intimately bound up with defining priorities and allocating resources.

Theories of 'need'

At a general level, two very different approaches to defining need exist in the literature. One approach is based on the notion that there are objective or universal human needs. Doyal and Gough (1991), for example, define these broadly in terms of physical survival and personal autonomy. However, while few would argue that there are basic needs for economic and physical security, accommodation, food, clothing and social relationships that must be met in a civilised society, there is a relative dimension to need also. Thus, what is seen as adequate in terms of meeting basic needs, and the means through which they can be appropriately met, will vary over time, both historically and over the life course, as well as across different cultures. This understanding has led to a focus on the relative nature of need.

Bradshaw (1972) makes a distinction between different dimensions of need on the basis of whether they are user, professionally or comparatively defined. From this perspective, 'user need' may be either expressed in terms of demand for particular services or felt in the context of a person's experiences and expectations. Professionally defined or 'normative need' is that determined by 'experts' or service agencies. 'Comparative need' is understood with reference to the level of resources and benefits available to similar others.

Smith (1980) also developed a relative conception of need. He suggests that, in the context of social care, need is in large part that which is defined by practitioners and others who are charged with meeting it. The issue for him is to examine how need is managed in practice within an agency. This will be determined by such factors as: the structure and organisation of the agency, including how accessible it is; the eligibility criteria operating; professional ideology; and the practical constraints within which workers operate.

Espousal of a relative conception of need in respect of social care does not in itself accord primacy to policy, agency or professional conceptions of need over against user views. It does, however, place the emphasis on the socially constructed nature of need. Two broad lines of enquiry flow from this understanding. First, it is important to explore how need is practically understood and managed within social care agencies. Second, one has to consider how users' understanding of need is shaped by their experiences and expectations, their views about what is right and proper to seek help about, and their knowledge of and access to services. To simply counterpose 'need' (that which is seen as legitimate by agencies/professionals) to 'wants' (how users perceive 'need') is not only overly simplistic. It also fails to treat as problematic policy and agency perspectives on need. But it is precisely because ideas of need are centrally bound up with resource allocation and prioritisation that the question of how need is shaped and defined, and whose needs are accorded legitimacy, are political and not just theoretical questions. It seems important, therefore, that, in order to understand need and unmet need, we critically examine the notions and assumptions underpinning conceptions of need at policy, service and practice level, in the first instance. We then proceed to explore need from the perspective of service users, with particular focus on the experiences of older people. It is our contention that the definitions of need, held variously within policy, in service agencies, through professional practice and by older people themselves, represent different but interacting ways of thinking about need, and of determining approaches to and evaluating outcomes.

Community care: the centrality and ambiguity of 'need' in policy

A fundamental policy thrust of the community care 'revolution', enshrined in the NHS and Community Care Act 1990, was to achieve a shift from a service-driven to a needs-led approach to assessment and service provision. This was seen as having two distinct though related aspects. First, it involved assessing the care needs of the local population, through the development of Community Care Plans. The construction of such plans not only envisaged partnership with voluntary and statutory agencies. It also intended that consultative processes would be developed to give voice to how people locally defined their needs.

The second aspect related to assessment and care management in respect of individual users and, latterly, their caregivers. Here, there was explicit emphasis on moving away from fitting people into existing services towards involving users and their caregivers centrally in decision making about what services should be provided and their mode of delivery. The focus then was on individually tailored packages of care.

However, at the core of the conception of need underpinning the reforms were the following.

- Need was defined with reference to agency policies, priorities and resources (Social Services Inspectorate/Department of Health, 1991). Thus, the responsibility of local authorities to meet need was limited to the resources available to them. This view of need was subsequently accorded legitimacy in the House of Lords ruling that Gloucestershire County Council could withdraw services it said it could no longer afford from a man who had previously been assessed as needing them.

- For older people in particular, the emphasis was on promoting the development of services to enable those at risk of institutional admission to remain in the community. Thus, need was limited and targeted towards enabling those older people on the threshold of institutional care to remain in their own homes for as long as possible. The implication was that the needs of those who were not at immediate risk would not be acknowledged or met.

- The concept of a needs-led service was intimately bound up with promoting user choice through the development of a mixed economy of care. It is evident, however, that the option of choosing between different providers does not in itself expand the opportunities available to people. What is required is that different kinds of care models are offered across a range of settings that meet user conceptions of quality provision.

- Needs should not be circumscribed by agency boundaries. Here, there was explicit focus on the fact that health and social care needs were inextricably tied in with people's social and emotional lives (e.g. physical and social environment, social isolation) and that need could not be categorised as 'social' or 'medical'. What has become increasingly problematic, however, is that the boundary around what are conceived of as health needs has become more tightly prescribed. This has occurred in the context that social care services have to be paid for, and access depends on a test of financial means. Health care, on the other hand, is free at the point of delivery.

Within the community care reforms, the language of 'need' has been central. At the same time, the conception of need articulated in policy has been inextricably bound up with rationing, cost containment and the increasing targeting of social services on those deemed to be very dependent. These tensions at policy level have been experienced most acutely at the point of implementation and practice.

Unmet need – the experience of community care implementation

Even within the framework of the narrow conception of need articulated within the community care reforms, there is considerable unmet need. To highlight just a number of these areas:

- There exists considerable variation in range, type and quality of service provision, and eligibility criteria, within and between local authorities (see, for example, Levin et al. [1994] on respite care services for older people with dementia; Godfrey et al. [2000] on home care provision). Much more needs to be done to document this variation.

- Because of the emphasis on cost containment, many local authorities are capping the costs of community care packages to those of residential/nursing home care, narrowing choice (Audit Commission, 1996). Similarly, there is variation in charging policies and service costs across authorities.

- Research that has focused on people with similar types of need suggests a potentially enormous gap between need, demand and service provision, indicating fruitful areas for further exploration. For example, secondary analysis of the Office of Population Censuses and Surveys (OPCS) Survey of Disability (Schneider et al., 1993) reveals that, while most people with moderate to severe dementia living in the community see their GP, only a small proportion (24 per cent) have a home help, and even fewer attend a day centre (12 per cent). While this predates the community care reforms, more recent community-based studies come to similar conclusions, albeit in the context of considerable local variation (Burholt et al., 1997, MRC CFAS and RIS MRC CFAS, 1999).

- Access to assessment is limited by agency definitions of risk (Rummery and Glendinning, 1999). Risk tends to be defined in terms of severity of disability and the lack of availability of an informal caregiver. This has implications for who gets into the service system in the first place, the nature of the assessment process (see below) and the extent to which caregiver needs are prioritised.

- Assessment systems and practices are dominated by a focus on physical and mental impairments, and a lack of attention paid to the emotional components of need or the meaning for older people themselves of what it means to be dependent (e.g. Godfrey and Moore, 1995; Clark et al., 1996). Yet, the levels of physical or mental disabilities of older people may not in themselves predict need for care. It is notable that a study carried out to examine the factors influencing the admission of older people to residential care found that there was not a simple link between dependency and admission (Department of Health, 1994). A key difference between those who remained at home and those who were admitted was not the level of impairment but the sheer determination of the former not to go into care. Qualitative research with black elders (Groger, 1994) revealed similar findings. Those remaining at home struggled for independence and were determined to define themselves as competent.

- Co-ordination of assessments/care plans is ineffective (Social Services Inspectorate, 1999). Users and carers experience frustration and see themselves as badly served by fragmented approaches from health and social care (Social Services Inspectorate, 1997). Social services care managers are often unaware of medical conditions that can lie behind functional disability; primary health care team members are slow to accept that some disability in older people may be improved by multi-disciplinary care packages (Health Advisory Service, 1997). There is considerable under-identification of such mental health problems as depression among older people, including those receiving social services help (for example, Banerjee and Macdonald, 1996; Schneider, 1997). There is evidence of a strong interrelationship between mental health problems, physical disability and poor social networks, leading to the conclusion that a combination of strategies spanning treatment and support is likely to be required (Alexopoulus, 1996).

- There is a failure to recognise the interactive nature of the needs of users and carers, and to focus on caregiving in old age primarily as a burden (Nolan et al., 1996). This does not take account of the fact that caregiving occurs in the framework of a relationship; that it often involves reciprocal help; and that older people are themselves a main source of help to others, for example spouses (O'Connor et al., 1989; Wenger, 1990).

These points can be summarised to suggest three main ways in which services fail to match need defined in service terms: *inequity*, where localities or groups with greater need do not have proportionally more services; *inadequacy*, where the services people *do* get are not always relevant to their need, or do not meet need in an effective, efficient or acceptable manner; and *fragmentation*, where failure to take a holistic approach leads to inadequate assessment and gaps and overlaps in provision.

Professional conceptions of need

It is notable that early attempts by professionals and local authorities to develop user-centred approaches to need assessment stemmed from the understanding that identifying need was not a simple question of asking people what they wanted. Rather, it was seen to involve a complex and negotiated process. This is because people's conceptions of their needs relate to their expectations, their view of what the agency can and should provide, what it is legitimate to ask for and their knowledge of the services that are available. There are, therefore, several layers of felt need on the part of older people that may not be expressed in requests for a service. These include the following.

- Needs are not expressed because people do not define them in service terms. For example, relatives of those in the early stages of dementia who are unsure as to what the problem is may delay seeking help (Askham, 1995). They may also be under pressure to deny the illness since the implications for the future may be too painful to acknowledge.

- Needs are not expressed because the services available are not considered appropriate. This is a specific problem experienced by black and minority ethnic elders (Boneham *et al.*, 1997). Other barriers to needs not being expressed include the quality of the service being perceived as poor (for example, respite provided within hospital wards or long-stay residential care homes).

Further to this are levels of engagement with services that reflect identified but unmet need:

- Service users who do not receive sufficient or appropriate services.

- Non-service users experiencing barriers to access. Again, in respect of dementia, there is a considerable amount of research indicating an array of internal and external obstacles encountered on the path to service provision (Pollitt *et al.*, 1991). This is exacerbated by the fact that professionals in over-stretched services often do not renew the offer of help that was initially rebuffed by older people and their carers because of concern about losing their independence at a later stage.

The recognition that need is socially constructed was reflected in imaginative attempts at involving users in the assessment process, during the early stages of community care implementation. For example, the biographical approach to need assessment (Johnson *et al.*, 1988) was based on the view that need had to be set in the context of people's lives, what was important to them, what they valued. The model of need assessment for young people with disabilities evaluated by Dowling *et al.* (1993) was based on the assumption that assessment involved a process of understanding the young person while simultaneously offering an opportunity to broaden their horizons and expand their expectations. The exchange model of assessment (Smale and Tuson, 1993) envisaged a situation where the professional negotiated with the user to obtain agreement about the support required and who was going to provide it. Drawing on the experience of the community care demonstration projects, Challis *et al.* (1995) pointed to the fact that assessment involved engaging the person and forming a relationship with them. This was the basis of both understanding their needs and securing their trust in accepting services. These conceptions of need envisaged an expansive, creative and interactive approach to assessment. It does appear, however, that the purchaser–provider split and cost containment has had a major impact on the content of assessment and care management. Thus, Ramcharan *et al.* (1999), from a survey in Wales, found that, while the administrative workload of practitioners increased considerably with the introduction of care management, time spent with users declined leading to the risk of routinised and unimaginative ways of working.

Service conceptions of need

Given resource shortfalls, most ways of thinking about need have been preoccupied with issues of resource allocation and the eligibility criteria that determine distribution. With regard to older people, too, service conceptions of need are underpinned by taken-for-granted, unreflective assumptions. It is accepted that the central concern of older people in terms of maintaining independence is to remain in their own homes and avoid going into residential care. But does this always apply? Is there a point at which the struggle to remain at home becomes too great? What do we know about older people's own perceptions in this regard?

It is also argued that older people prefer to rely on family and friends as they become more dependent, and only in the final resort do they seek help from outside agencies. Yet, there are some indications from research that attitudes and expectations of older people in terms of care preferences may be changing. West *et al.* (1984), for example, found that most people were unwilling to place the major burden of care on their immediate families. Morris (1994) found that, for many of the people with disabilities in her study, receiving help from sources outside the family and those intimate was crucial in maintaining a relationship of equality. From this perspective, help from formal agencies can be perceived not as dependency but as a resource that can facilitate maintaining interdependence and reciprocity within informal relationships. Being in a position to give and not only receive help is important to older people. Wenger (1992), in the context of rural North Wales, found that, at low levels of dependency, older people generally were confident of getting help from friends and neighbours in the knowledge that they could and would reciprocate. At higher levels of dependency, where people needed regular help with domestic tasks and personal care, they turned to family members. Thus, access to kin, particularly close family members, determines who gets what care. It also appears that there are social class differences operating in respect of the nature of the social networks that older people have (Phillipson *et al.*, 1998). Similarly, normative obligations around caregiving may vary between ethnic groups (Finch and Mason, 1990). Several key questions are therefore posed.

- What sorts of need and preferences for care and support do people have now?
- How do these vary in terms of geography, culture, ethnicity and social class, and with different levels of loss (physical, social, emotional)?
- What is the distribution of these needs and preferences within the population, and how is this changing?
- Which of these needs and preferences can and should public services meet?
- How good is the match between the pattern of current services and the pattern of need?
- How could the pattern of current services be changed to better meet need and user preferences?

Redefining need

In developing a user conception of need, it is important to start from the lived experiences of older people. Thus, the framework within which the needs of older people are understood is not bound by the view of older people as burden or as passive bystanders in their own lives. This approach is intended to consider user need in a way that can form the basis for creative rethinking. The questions posed must be expansive and inclusive rather than merely more discussions about the adequacy of existing provision. The purpose is to bring issues, which have not thus far played a major part in the policy agenda, into the debate.

We have identified that need is, at least in part, socially constructed. Thus, user conceptions of need are not static but shift and change with reference to experiences and expectations. They can be understood only in the context of people's life history – the conditions and the times through which they have lived, the difficulties they have encountered and resolved, the unresolved issues they carry with them and the meaning they give to these. Ageing per se does not turn people into different beings; rather, there is continuity of self and self-esteem despite the generally negative attitude to ageing that many older people share (Coleman et al., 1993, 1998). At the same time, older people do not comprise a homogeneous group. On the contrary, what is important is the diversity of old age.

The view of ageing as being about loss and decline has been challenged by the conception that it also involves adjustment, self-esteem and growth. Baltes and Carstensen (1996) argue that these different perspectives can be reconciled within a model that characterises the ageing process as a changing balance between gains and losses that become less positive with age. Managing this changing balance involves a complex process of adaptation to physical, social, interpersonal and psychological losses that tend to accompany ageing. While the mechanisms to achieve this successfully over the life course are not fully understood, a number of factors have been identified as important. First, there is management of the limitations in one's physical or other abilities. Second, there is a redirection of effort to maintain and improve competence in those areas that are valued. Third, there are attempts to develop new strategies (both those internal to the individual, or within the social or physical environment) to compensate for losses. These linked processes – selection, compensation and optimisation – operate to manage ageing successfully, i.e. in the sense of attaining valued goals, minimising losses and maximising gains (Baltes and Baltes, 1990). Adaptation to loss then embraces both learning and adjustment through which people are active participants. Even so, what are perceived as valued goals to pursue and the kinds of strategies adopted will be shaped and constrained by the resources available to the individual (for example, socio-economic, situation and social support networks) and the expectations, normative obligations and roles attached to being and becoming old. Moreover, people have differential access to resources as they age.

While viewing older people as a homogenous group acknowledges important common factors in ageing which shape current experience, the perspective ignores the pre-existing divisions *within* the group that mean that the impact of those factors will not be uniform. For the most part, social policy deals with ageing as a period of frailty. Yet, the experiences of older people, including their health and life chances, are mediated through inequalities based on class, gender and ethnicity. Indeed, for more affluent older people, many of the deleterious experiences of ageing may be circumvented, minimised or delayed (Jerome, 1993).

Research studies that have focused on the experiences of older people demonstrate both the losses encountered in old age and how people respond to the challenges. For example, Thompson (1992) and Pickard (1995) have pointed to the active role some older people take following bereavement, both in terms of taking part in social activities and developing new relationships and friendships. Pickard (1995) from her study in a close-knit community found that women seemed better at drawing on friendships with other women, developing new contacts and activities; whereas men seemed to experience more difficulties. Similarly, Thompson (1992) has shown that, despite severe limitations of activity, most of the older people studied developed coping strategies and modifed their lifestyle to take into account these restrictions. There is evidence too to suggest that successful adaptation depends on maintaining involvement in specific areas of life either because of their symbolic significance (Wenger, 1992) or their importance in maintaining self-esteem (Coleman *et al.*, 1998). Wenger (1992) found that for many older people the high value attached to shopping, cooking and gardening, for example, reflected the opportunities they afforded for social contact, the outlets for creativity they offered and the demonstration of continued competence that they represented. Continued participation in these activities was perceived as crucial to older people's conception of independence. Conversely, maintaining involvement in such tasks as housework and property maintenance was not seen as so central to the person's sense of identity (though there are likely to be gender differences here). From this perspective, need should be considered in terms of services that facilitate older people's continued participation in valued activities. Thus a need-based service response would be geared towards sustaining involvement in those activities that people find pleasure in doing or that are central to their perception of themselves as competent.

Exploring unmet need

Close relationships and social networks are central to the experience of well-being in later life. What also appears key is that such relationships are based not only on affection but also on reciprocity. Coleman *et al.* (1998) pointed to the value attached by older people to providing as well as receiving help and support. Hockey and James (1993) suggested that the notion of one-way help as between the carer and cared for person can produce a loss of social power as well as personal control on the part of the cared for individual. In reality, focus on the experience of caregiving in the context of a relationship as opposed to an emphasis on the tasks undertaken by 'carers' indicates that in the main the flow of support is not a one-way street (Nolan *et al.*, 1996). At the same time, older people are a substantial source of care for vulnerable relatives (e.g. Arber and Ginn, 1990; Levin *et al.*, 1994).

For older people, maintaining continuity of place (in the sense of their own home and community) assumes considerable importance. Not only has it associations with family, friends and past memories, it offers a familiar environment within which to negotiate increasing disabilities. Means (1997) argues that housing is the foundation of community care and places emphasis on strategies and services to enable older people to remain in their own homes. Victor (1987), in a review of research on sheltered housing, found that such schemes had only a marginal impact on tenants' perceptions of loneliness, and many looked outside of the physical confines of the scheme to family and previous friends for much of their social contact.

Finally, one of the most damaging threats to older people is a loss of life purpose and boredom.

The focus on ageing as a process of learning and adjustment in which older people themselves are actively involved in developing their own coping strategies lays the foundation for an empowering rather than dependency-based conception of need. It lays bare the degree to which older people have the power to define a 'good' old age for themselves. The implications of this approach for assessing unmet need are that it begins with older people's definitions and not from the service provider perspective.

Needs are then constructed in terms of:

- intimate and social relationships based on notions of reciprocity
- maintaining a sense of purpose, meaning and competence
- being able to retain involvement in valued aspects of life
- engagement in meaningful activities
- retaining continuity with place and relationships
- sufficient income
- practical, social, personal care in ways that ensure autonomy and sense of control.

The content and quality of service provision then require focus on supporting attainment and satisfaction of these needs. Some of the questions this poses include the following.

- How do we understand what constitutes dignified ageing and how can services operate to support and enhance this?
- What do independence, dependence and interdependence mean? In an ideology of independence, how do we achieve dignity for those who must be dependent? What forms of collective interdependence might support and meet people's needs?
- What are the emotional impacts of dependency? What does it mean to be a recipient of care? How can care be provided in ways that do not reinforce people's sense of being incompetent?

These are questions that take us beyond a concern with meeting physical need only towards addressing other equally important components of need, based on social participation and emotional involvement. They are qualitative questions which concern *how* need is met. Only when these dimensions of experience are understood can we go on to explore how felt need may be turned into a dialogue with policy makers and service providers.

The conceptualisation of need within the framework of citizenship offers one approach to recognising need in terms of social participation. Marshall (1950) distinguished between civil, legal and social forms of citizenship, while also pointing to the interrelationship between rights and needs across these areas. Thus, one has to be able to exercise social citizenship to make legal and political citizenship have any meaning. If we cannot participate in society because of the lack of support to meet our social needs, and mitigate physical disability or illness, we may also be excluded from taking a real part in the democratic processes of society or from exercising our legal rights.

The process of determining felt need should be seen as an interactive one between citizens and services in a relationship of negotiation rather than one of provider and recipient. This poses a major reorientation of services and requires a consideration of the following.

- A shift from an individualised conception of welfare towards a collectivist model of service provision: social services currently operate a predominantly individual (social pathology) model of service. While recent policy initiatives place more emphasis on community development, these have tended to develop outside of mainstream social work (e.g. Better Government for Older People Initiative). A collective model of service provision, on the other hand, would place focus on need in terms of autonomy and self-determination rather than on a residual and stigmatised notion of welfare.

- Assessment as a process of facilitation and negotiation, starting from people's lived experience: in practice, this might suggest, for example, the care management role as doing *with* instead of *to* or *for* (Lymbery, 1998).

- User involvement in determining what is acceptable risk: this also embraces the user's confidence in being able to decide, or allowing others to decide, what risks can and should be taken. At an individual level, personal control and confidence can determine the trajectory and experience of ageing.

The future agenda

From the discussion of need undertaken thus far, we can draw out a number of conclusions about a range of issues significant in determining current definitions of need.

- Needs are defined in terms of the predominant social and cultural values of the time.
- Current society engenders low expectations for self and others in old age.
- The welfare state is unable to identify, address and respond to many needs.
- Personal aspirations are influenced by service perspectives.

- Professionals have power to define need in service and organisational terms.
- Need is usually defined in terms of demand for existing services.

Current definitions of need that are employed to manage demand on services may not be open to a simple process of challenge and redefinition. Because they have become institutionalised in organisational and professional understandings and practice, they must be subjected to scrutiny for any real orientation to take place. An example here is the way support with housework tasks has been redefined by many local authority social services departments as being outside of their remit to provide.

Organisational constraints that shape how need is defined in service and professional terms include:

- resource availability – cash limits, policy and priorities
- organisational structures and responsibilities – duties and powers, policy and priorities within services and agencies, for example, what is 'medical' and what is 'social' need
- intra-organisational barriers and boundaries – the right hand not working with the left, etc.
- inter-organisational gaps and overlaps.

Professional responses to need are shaped by ideology, culture, policy and organisational factors such as:

- value base
- clinical governance
- legislation and litigation

- education and training
- peer group influence.

For example, professional practice and the legislative framework mean that occupational therapists may safely lift and handle people with appropriate training, whereas nurses and care workers may not, insisting that people accept a hoist even if that is not their preference.

What is problematic, however, is that, from the perspective of maintaining autonomy and dignity in old age, these organisational and professional practices result in costs in not preventing unnecessary dependence, while also lowering people's quality of life.

In redefining need, we can begin with knowledge based on evidence drawn from the experience of older people, some elements of which have been set out above. This knowledge is not of uniform quality and there remain some gaps. It sets out a starting point that requires further development.

The agenda for research and practice

The burden of this paper has been to argue that, in terms of understanding need in respect of older people, we need to develop an agenda that can explore the socially constructed and therefore the continually changing nature of need. At the same time, it argues that one should start from the lived experience of older people and not from how need is conceptualised in policy and practice. From these considerations flow some questions that require further exploration for research and practice.

Developing a research and practice agenda

The research agenda should be constructed with, and in relation to, those issues and concerns perceived as salient by older people themselves. From what is known from the albeit limited evidence base, these would include the following.

- Examining how older people themselves manage the losses and limitations that accompany ageing.
- Exploring the conflicts and incongruities between service definitions of need, practice and older people's conceptions of quality of life.
- Exploring the gaps between need, demand and provision of service by looking at those who receive and those who do not receive formal support.
- Developing understanding and support for independence and interdependence as well as dignified dependence.
- Examining how ageing represents continuity and discontinuity over the life course as well as the critical transition points.
- Understanding the impact of inequality in access to services as well as how it shapes conceptions of need.

A number of issues pertinent to practice can also be identified:

- Broadening the agenda of education and health promotion to challenge low expectations and strengthen aspiration and demand.
- Developing tools for self-management programmes.
- Continuing pressure for partnership in action in whole systems ways – across the public and independent sectors, and organisational and professional boundaries.

- Developing and broadening the prevention agenda.

- Developing user-centred processes and creating a dialogue between those with a legitimate interest in defining need.

These principles for research and practice are suggested as a way of maintaining focus on both the absolute and the socially constructed dimensions of need identified earlier in this paper. In pursuing these questions, we can make visible the political judgements inherent in many, ostensibly neutral, practice- and service-based approaches. Such an approach, we would argue, is the necessary starting point for generating a more fundamental reorientation in policy, which can begin with older people's definition of need.

REFERENCES

Alexopoulos, G. (1996) 'Editorial: geriatric depression in primary care', *International Journal of Geriatric Psychiatry*, Vol. 11, pp. 397–400

Arber, S. and Ginn, J. (1990) 'The meaning of informal care: gender and the contribution of elderly people', *Ageing and Society*, Vol. 10, No. 4, pp. 429–54

Askham, J. (1995) 'Making sense of dementia: carers' perceptions', *Ageing and Society*, Vol. 15, No. 1, pp. 103–14

Audit Commission (1996) 'Balancing the care equation: progress with care in the community', *Community Care Bulletin 3*. London: HMSO

Audit Commission (1997) *The Coming of Age: Improving Care Services for Older People*. London: The Stationery Office

Baldock, J. (1997) 'Social care in old age: more than a funding problem', *Social Policy and Administration*, Vol. 31, No. 1, pp. 73–89

Baltes, M.M. and Carstensen, L.L. (1996) 'The process of successful ageing', *Ageing and Society*, Vol. 16, No. 4, pp. 397–421

Baltes, P.B. and Baltes, M.M. (1990) 'Psychological perspectives on successful ageing: the model of selective optimization with compensation', in P.B. Baltes and M.M. Baltes (eds) *Successful Ageing: Perspectives from the Behavioural Sciences*. New York: Cambridge University Press, pp. 1–34

Banerjee, S. and Macdonald, A. (1996) 'Mental disorder in an elderly home care population: associations with health and social services use', *British Journal of Psychiatry*, Vol. 168, pp. 760–6

Boneham, M.A., Williams, K.E. and Copeland, J.R.M. (1997) 'Elderly people from ethnic minorities in Liverpool: mental illness, unmet need and barriers to service use', *Health and Social Care in the Community*, Vol. 5, No. 3, pp. 173–80

Bradshaw, J. (1972) 'A taxonomy of social need', in G. McLachlan (ed.) *Problems and Progress in Medical Care*. Oxford: Oxford University Press

Burholt, V., Wenger, C. and Scott, A. (1997) 'Dementia, disability and contact with formal services: a comparison of dementia sufferers and non-sufferers in rural and urban settings', *Health and Social Care in the Community*, Vol. 5, No. 6, pp. 384–97

References

Challis, D., Darton, R. and Johnson, L. (1995) *Care Management and Health Care of Older People*. Aldershot: Ashgate Publishing

Clark, H., Dyer, S. and Hartman, L. (1996) *Going Home: Older People Leaving Hospital*. Bristol: The Policy Press

Coleman, P.G., Ivani-Chalian, C. and Robinson, M. (1993) 'Self-esteem and its sources: stability and change in later life', *Ageing and Society*, Vol. 13, No. 2, pp. 171–92

Coleman, P., Ivani-Chalian, C. and Robinson, M. (1998) 'The story continues: persistence of life themes in old age', *Ageing and Society*, Vol. 18, No. 4, pp. 398–419

Department of Health (1994) *The F Factor: Reasons why some Older People Choose Residential Care*. London: Department of Health

Dowling, M., Phillips, D., Walker, A. and Godfrey, M. (1993) *Assessment of the Needs of Young People with Disabilities*. Hounslow: London Borough of Hounslow

Doyal, L. and Gough, I. (1991) *A Theory of Human Needs*. Basingstoke: Macmillan

Finch, J. and Mason, J. (1990) 'Filial obligations and kin support for elderly people', *Ageing and Society*, Vol. 10, No. 2, pp. 151–75

Godfrey, M. and Moore, J. (1995) *Hospital Discharge: User, Carer and Professional Perspectives*. Leeds: Nuffield Institute for Health, University of Leeds

Godfrey, M., Randall, T., Long, A. and Grant, M. (2000) *Home Care: a Review of Effectiveness and Outcomes*. Exeter: Centre of Evidence-based Social Work

Groger, L. (1994) 'Limit of support and reaction to illness: an exploration of black elders' pathways to long term care settings', *Journal of Cross Cultural Gerontology*, Vol. 9, No. 4, pp. 369–87

Hancock, R. (1998) 'Housing wealth, income and financial wealth of older people in Britain', *Ageing and Society*, Vol. 18. No. 1, pp. 5–33

Health Advisory Service (1997) *Services for People who are Elderly: Addressing the Balance*. London: The Stationery Office

Hockey, J. and James, A. (1993) *Growing up and Growing old: Ageing and Dependency in the Life Course*. London: Sage Publications

Jerome, D. (1993) 'Intimate relationships', in J. Bond, P. Coleman and S. Peace (eds) *Ageing in Society: an Introduction to Social Gerontology*. London: Sage Publications

Johnson, M., Gearing, B., Carley, M. and Dant, T. (1988) *A Biographically Based Health and Social Diagnostic Technique: a Research Report*. Buckingham and London: The Open University and Policy Studies Institute

Levin, E., Moriarty, J. and Gorbach, P. (1994) *Better for the Break*. London: HMSO

Lymbery, M. (1998) 'Care management and professional autonomy: the impact of community care legislation on social work with older people', *British Journal of Social Work*, Vol. 28, No. 6, pp. 863–78

Marshall, T.H. (1950) *Citizenship and Social Class and Other Essays*. Cambridge: Cambridge University Press

Means, R. (1997) 'Home, independence and community care: time for a wider vision?', *Policy and Politics*, Vol. 25, No. 4, pp. 409–19

Morris, J. (1994) 'Community care or independent living', *Critical Social Policy*, Vol. 40, pp. 24–44

MRC CFAS and RIS MRC CFAS (1999) 'Profile of disability in elderly people: estimates from a longitudinal population study', *British Medical Journal*, Vol. 318: pp. 1108–11

Nolan M., Grant, G. and Keady, J. (1996) *Understanding Family Care*. Buckingham: Open University Press

O'Connor, D.W., Pollitt, P.A., Brook, C. and Reiss, B.B. (1989) 'The distribution of services to demented elderly people living in the community', *International Journal of Geriatric Psychiatry*, Vol. 4, pp. 339–44

Phillipson, C., Bernard, H., Phillips, J. and Ogg, J. (1998) 'The family and community life of older people: household composition and social networks in three urban areas', *Ageing and Society*, Vol. 18, No. 3, pp. 259–89

Pickard, S. (1995) *Living on the Front Line: a Social Anthropological Study of Old Age and Ageing*. Aldershot: Avebury

Pollitt, P., Anderson, I. and O'Connor, D.W. (1991) 'For better or for worse: the experience of caring for an early dementing spouse', *Ageing and Society*, Vol. 11. No. 4, pp. 443–69

Ramcharan, P., Grant, G., Parry-Jones, B. and Robinson, C. (1999) 'The roles and tasks of care management practitioners in Wales revisited', *Managing Community Care*, Vol. 7, No. 3, pp. 29–36

Rummery, K. and Glendinning, C. (1999) 'Negotiating needs, access and gatekeeping: developments in health and community care policies in the UK and the rights of disabled and older citizens', *Critical Social Policy*, Vol. 19, No. 3, pp. 335–51

Schneider, J. (ed.) (1997) *Quality of Care: Testing some Measures in Homes for Elderly People*. Discussion Paper 1245. Canterbury: Personal Social Services Research Unit, University of Kent

Schneider, J., Kavanagh, S. and Knapp, M. (1993) 'Elderly people with advanced cognitive impairment in England: resources, use and costs', *Ageing and Society*, Vol. 13, pp. 27–50

References

Smale, G. and Tuson, G. (1993) *Empowerment, Assessment, Care Management and the Skilled Worker*. London: National Institute of Social Work

Smith, G. (1980) *Social Need*. London: Routledge and Kegan Paul

Social Services Inspectorate/Department of Health (1991) *Care Management and Assessment: the Practitioners' Guide*. London: HMSO

Social Services Inspectorate (1997) *The Cornerstone of Care: Inspection of Care Planning for Older People*. London: Department of Health

Social Services Inspectorate (1999) *Of Primary Importance: Inspection of Social Services Departments' Links with Primary Health Services*. London: Department of Health

Thompson, P. (1992) '"I don't feel old": subjective ageing and the search for meaning in later life', *Ageing and Society*, Vol. 12, No. 1, pp. 23–48

Victor, C.R. (1987) *Old Age in Modern Society: a Textbook of Social Gerontology*. London: Croom Helm

Wenger, C. (1990) 'Elderly carers: the need for appropriate intervention', *Ageing and Society*, Vol. 10, No. 2, pp. 197–219

Wenger, C. (1992) *Help in Old Age: Facing up to Change*. Liverpool: Liverpool University Press

West, P., Illsley, R. and Kelman, H. (1984) 'Public preferences for the care of dependency groups', *Social Science and Medicine*, Vol. 18, pp. 417–46